Creatures of Promise

Creatures of Promise

Poems by

Mary Junge

© 2024 Mary Junge. All rights reserved.
This material may not be reproduced in any form, published,
reprinted, recorded, performed, broadcast,
rewritten or redistributed without
the explicit permission of Mary Junge.
All such actions are strictly prohibited by law.

Cover design by Shay Culligan
Cover photo by Mark Matasovsky
Author photo by Jacqueline Kayleigh Photography

ISBN: 978-1-63980-517-4

Kelsay Books
502 South 1040 East, A-119
American Fork, Utah 84003
Kelsaybooks.com

for Mark

Acknowledgments

Thanks to the editors of the publications who first published the following poems, some in slightly different versions:

Bluefire (Laurel Poetry Collective): "Prairie Grass"

Body of Evidence (Laurel Poetry Collective): "Lek," "View from the Caroni Swamp, Trinidad," "Indigo Bunting"

bosque: "Birds"

Crosswinds Poetry Journal: "Watching My Mother Smoke," "Sonnet for Time"

Oyster River Pages: "Dog Park, Ocean Beach, San Diego"

Rag Queen: "Mother's Five-Year Diary"

Red Wing Poet Artist Collaboration Chapbook: "Summer Doesn't Last"

Split Rock Review: "In My Backyard"

Thanks to Karen Kelsay, Delisa Hargrove, Jenna Wray, and the talented team of editors and designers at Kelsay Books for publishing this collection of poems.

Contents

I.

Summer Doesn't Last	15
Birds	16
Lek	17
View from the Caroni Swamp, Trinidad	18
Night Walk, Tambopata River, Peru	19
Indigo Bunting	20
Like Promises	21
The Sandhill Cranes Stop in Minnetonka	22
Birds in Hiding	23
Coupling	24
Prairie Grass	25
Morning of the Blood Moon	26
Game Drives, Botswana	27
In My Backyard	28
As the Forests Burn	29
Ode to the Banyan Tree of Lahaina, Maui	30
The Wild Horses of Sardinia	31
Remembering the Brown Recluse Spider	32
Where the Deer Slept	33
Anagram for War	34
The Norwegian Resistance Museum, Akershus Fortress, Oslo	35
The Leafcutter Ants of Trinidad	36
Putting the Roses to Bed	37

II.

Turning Pages	41
Rituals	42
On the Occasion of My Birth	43
My Mother Was a School Librarian	44

Watching My Mother Smoke	45
Mother's Five-Year Diary	46
Liza Lou's Kitchen	48
Early Photo of My Father	49
The Rat Snake	50
The Genealogist and Horses	51
My Father's Circles	52
She Liked to Tell Strangers She Was Adopted	53
Lost Days and Nights, Part I	54
Lost Days and Nights, Part II	55
Like Conjoined Twins	56
This Is the Story of a Stranger	57
Long Shadows	58
American Sonnet, the Body	59
Elegy for My Sister	60
Love Poem for North Dakota	61

III.

Sonnet for Time	65
The List	66
Artifacts	67
Clothes on the Line	68
Microchimera	69
My Suspicious Breast	70
Oropesa, Spain, Where Pilgrims Once Slept	72
Husbands	73
In the Therapy Pool	74
The Painter in His Studio	76
At the Butterfly Museum	77
Dog Park, Ocean Beach, San Diego	78
It Keeps Happening in Minneapolis	79
The Eagle Cam	80

Sugaring	82
The Small Paintbox of April	83
Mother, the hummingbirds arrived	84
Dark Night with a Strawberry Moon	85
Like labor pains	86
Love All of It	87

I.

Summer Doesn't Last

after James Wright

It comes while you're splashing in lake water like a seal
or when your head is down, after you've made
plans for June, July, and August.
It comes as you're savoring cold lemonade
with the right amount of sugar.
It comes like a speeding train carrying the blistering heat,
while you're driving north and counting roadkill:
deer, porcupines, foxes, and skunks.

It comes north of Bemidji as two skunks cross the road,
a baby hitching a ride on his mother's back.

The thing about summer is that it's never enough,
its end always just over the horizon.
You can't slow the Mississippi River or summer.
And your unruly garden?
You weed and weed until you see sunspots
but you can't keep up.

Summer always splits you open, so you remember
that you were born for this—pleasure.

Duffy's hammock hangs empty between two trees.
You can't go back. Winter is coming.

Birds

Year after year
the universe seems static.
Then, explosions,
fires, dark holes,
the skies gone quiet.

The skies gone quiet. An owl must be about.
A disturbance in one part offers itself to the whole.
A little yeast and sugar and wheat becomes bread,
spewing tiny bubbles of carbon dioxide, whose
particles float in space.

Particles float in space, like birds
who will nest on anything—the underside of a deck,
an abandoned barn, the used nest of other birds.
Hawks post high on electric poles over freeways
on the outskirts of cities, scavengers.

Scavengers, the Andean condors spread
their wide wings, whose tips resemble fingers,
ride the thermal currents
down and down
into the Colca.

Colca, the deepest canyon,
where we looked up from our ledge.
What sound did the condors make?
Deafened by fear,
I remember only how their wings shadowed us.

Their wings shadowed us.
Birds in flight shift sunlight,
the great condors, yes, and goldfinches too.
Even you make a shadow,
even I.

Lek

It's a singles bar for birds during mating season.
The female manakins ask two questions:
Can he dance? Does he keep his place clean?
We've heard that the males do handstands, and we're willing
to wait, as if we're having a Quaker meeting of three,
women suppressing laughter—impressed by the tales
of these tiny, bearded birds who never do show up.
No matter: It's May. The leatherback turtles
are arriving from afar to lay their eggs on the beaches
of Trinidad. Queen bees are taking their nuptial flights
and the orange Chaconia blossoms cry, *Look here, look here!*
The pink torch lilies and the ruddy ground dove say,
Love, love, love. Every morning the parrots shriek,
Hurry up! Seize the day! At night the pygmy owls repeat
their solemn question: *Who are you?*
Who are you?

View from the Caroni Swamp, Trinidad

There are birds that change you:
the scarlet ibises overhead at dusk,

all flying to the same island,
home for the night,

and a woman seated in a small boat,
now the only point of stillness.

Night Walk, Tambopata River, Peru

Were it not for our guide, who walked
these paths as a child, I would have missed
the sleeping white bird with her puffed-out,
red-tinged breast, wings tucked at rest,
perched on a low branch next to the trail.
Birds often sleep with an eye open,
brain half-awake, watchful.
Not she: Both eyes remained closed
as her breast lifted and fell in rapid rhythm.
She did not waken to our low voices
nor to Jorge's tiny red light.
We fell into a dark fold where time yawned.
If she could sleep as we stood watching her,
anything might be possible, the future
changed somehow, everything true.

Indigo Bunting

At first, I thought it was a bluebird,
the only blue bird I'd ever seen,
aside from the jay.
I wanted to shout out the word *blue,*
as if my cry could hold
the iridescence in place.

The rules of letting go are slippery.
In the end, we keep nothing.
Spectacular birds always take flight.
When I return to the place
where I saw the indigo bunting,
I find nothing there but myself,
my lonely self.

Like Promises

It's the surprise of birds I love most.
Yesterday, at Purgatory Park,
two long, narrow streaks appeared,
like disappearing yellow paint
between the newly green bushes.
The day before it was a block of red,
first hidden among the tall wet grass,
then soaring before I could whisper *cardinal*.
Today, out the south window, high in a maple,
a wood duck struggled (a juvenile?)
to find a way to land—
clumsy, for a bird so large
to nest so high.
Each day it goes like that,
never knowing which birds will show.
They come suddenly, full of grace.
As if they never read the news at all.

The Sandhill Cranes Stop in Minnetonka

Their squawking choruses like a flock,
but the calls come from only two birds
here at my favorite park with its meandering
creek and tall prairie grasses.
When one calls, the other joins in.

I study the red-masked creatures, poised
on tall, thin legs. *How is it possible*
for such legs to carry their great weight?

They rest and preen. The female
keeps her head down while the male stops
to look around, alert to distant barking dogs.

He twists and turns his Houdini neck
to reach his farthest tail feathers. He beak-combs
them again and again in ritual care
as my great-grandmother Martina Louise brushed
her long hair one hundred strokes each night.

Birds in Hiding

I cut the tall purple irises and bring them inside,
drop them into a crystal vase,
set them on the dining room table.
Again, the smell of summer rain.

Emotions go astray,
sadness over the spent apple blossoms
lining the streets. Nothing here
to be saved.

Yesterday, at the meeting, the baby's
face resembled a sunflower.
On the deck, five baby birds,
black-capped chickadees, in the birdhouse.

When their mother comes in with a worm
or goes out for another, their pleading voices
make a high chorus. After the last big storm, the bullfrogs
that had been keeping us awake at night suddenly quit.

It is dusk, raining again.
The green trees appear black against the fading blue.
They dance and rest, dance and rest. And the birds?
The birds we love so much have gone into hiding.

Coupling

The best chance for seeing birds comes early.
A mallard couple swims on the creek by the footbridge.
The woods vibrate high and low, enough to make me forget
our excesses, though earth's dominoes have begun to fall.
Yet, here are the wild turkeys fulfilling their promise.

The male spreads his fan wide. The female sits ready
for him to teeter on her back as she gets her massage
before their cloacal kiss, his deposit for the future.
Another female ambles by, interested,
but she will have to wait or find another partner.

I think how we were early in love, he in his lambchop sideburns
and me in my forest-green sweater, a gift from a former boyfriend.
How many years passed before my husband confessed
about his blacklight, how my white bra shined luminescent
through the stretched yarns that night?

Years later, walking with our children at the San Diego Zoo,
we passed a field of rhinos where a male was mounting a female,
setting his front feet upon her hindquarters carefully. Fifteen
hundred pounds spread evenly on each side.
It seemed he would crush her, yet she didn't move.

She was enjoying herself, and I enjoyed the spectacle
too, until our eldest complained, *Mom, come on!* I won't stop
watching the young couples on blankets by the lake,
dogs in heat, ducks rocking in the water and strutting on land,
red-bellied woodpeckers dipping their heads while singing

to each other, the male cardinal feeding the female,
multitudes of birds intent on collecting
what is needed for their nests, ready to improvise
with yarn, dryer lint, and bits of trash,
in answer to an ancient call.

Prairie Grass

Prairie grass shimmers surrounded by her many friends.
Each day she raises her thin stalk skyward.
When it is cloudy, she gives a hint of a wave
just before the clouds let go.
At night she whispers to the silent buffalo.
Prairie grass never needs approval or instruction.
Each fall she knows to seed the earth again
as the infant knows to smile soon after her perilous journey.

Morning of the Blood Moon

Return to the dazzle of zebras,
Savuti, Botswana.
Together they faced east
just after dawn in a sun salute.

Last night our sky touched the velvet sky
of Africa where the Milky Way is clearer.
Where the stars shine brighter
without the darkening wealth of our cities.

Game Drives, Botswana

Last night at dusk, two cheetah brothers worked together,
crouched in wait for a herd of impalas to pass,
then made chase, disappearing over a ridge,
only to return minutes later, defeated and hungry.
Even the great cheetah must fail and fail again.

We drive the maze of bumpy, narrow roads
while our guide talks on his radio, gathering clues
about the elusive leopard.
We are gamblers, all in, but time is running out:
It is nearly noon. We bounce along, eating road dust,
wearing boredom's dusky eyeshadow.

Our sleepy eyes startle awake. The leopard
we've been seeking runs beside us, inches from the tires
of our open jeep. Like silent owls, those of us seated
on the left turn our heads to look down
at him trotting beside us.
We are careful not to meet his eyes when he looks
up to glimpse our heads, shoulders, torsos.
Without legs, the guide tells us, *we are unrecognizable,
neither human nor animal.* For a little while we live
like that, the leopard's moving camouflage.

In My Backyard

The coyote looks free, running through the marsh
beside the creek, bottlebrush tail thick as a fireplace
broom swishing the cold air. At first, I take her
for one of the neighborhood dogs. Long ago,
I'd read about the Chicago coyotes who kept
their den by the stadium, where they followed
traffic lights and waited for cars to pass.
Here, they cover a few miles each day hunting:
cats, dogs, mice, rabbits, possums, moles, voles.
I saw one a couple of miles from here, too, at Purgatory
Park, where on that sunny morning she paused on the
snow-covered path, turning her head to meet my gaze,
as if posing a question I could never grasp.
Sure, I know, I should have waved my arms to make myself
seem bigger, to keep us from becoming too *familiar*.
But aren't we already *familiar,* neighbors as we are,
and equally fated with the weary walruses floating
on melting ice chunks in the ocean?

As the Forests Burn

We are praying for rain when the newscaster tells
of the two-year-old trampled outside the walls of Kabul Airport.
The girl's inconsolable mother could not save her from the crush.
Of what use are tears that never reach the burning forests?

Here, recklessness blooms and spreads like fire.
Today, on the freeway, speeding cars darted around mine.
Where were the state troopers?
Police continue killing our black and brown people.

After dark, citizens shoot each other. Last night, seven
took bullets on Lake Street.
I cannot stop the bullets ranging across my city.
What have we not yet ruined in this tired world?

I have no remedy for the bodies crushed
at the airport walls. When the planes departed Kabul,
desperate people clung to the wings,
rose up before falling, never changing into birds.

Ode to the Banyan Tree of Lahaina, Maui

We saw it for the first time in 1983.
Our toddler scaled the tree's above-ground roots
in his blue tennis shoes with gold laces,

wearing the prideful smile of a mountain climber,
his arms and hands extended up, as if in praise
to the aerial roots dangling near his head.

That was decades before our thermometers began rising,
when we still believed we'd always be able to travel,
free to seek the wonders of the world.

Last summer, we spent weeks indoors to avoid smoke
from the wildfires and other air pollutants. We hadn't yet seen
multiple fires converging to form one tornadic inferno.

On television we saw Lahaina turned to ash. My mother-in-law
would cry for the tree she visited every year for forty-five years.
For decades, lovers carved their names into the banyan's limbs,

and still it thrived. Days after the fire, volunteers formed a *hui*.
Soon, tanker trucks were dousing the banyan
with hundreds of gallons of water every few hours.

Then they began aerating the soil around the tree's roots,
feeding it compost tea and alfalfa, remedies on trial.
Now, weeks after the fire, new roots sprout from the old tree,

its branches reaching skyward in praise or prayer.

Note: A banyan sapling from India, eight feet tall, was planted in Lahaina in 1873 by the town sheriff to mark the fiftieth anniversary of the arrival of Protestant missionaries. Known for having aerial roots, the banyan thrived in Lahaina in its rich volcanic soil. Long considered to be Hawaii's symbol of hope, the tree is 150 years old and covers 1.93 acres. It is the largest banyan tree in the United States.

The Wild Horses of Sardinia

We walk far among the myrtle and cork trees in search
of the wild horses of Giara. These rugged paths lack signs.
The ranger offered directions as we entered the park,
but that was hours ago. Since then, we may have walked
through the poppy fields of Oz. We're not sure.

In the distance, the trees seem to stop.
We might be seeing mirages. We've been wrong twice before.
We trudge on, walk into a clearing, see water beyond
and crowfoot flowers covering the surface in wide,
irregular swaths, delicate white flowers with yellow centers.

Six horses stand in the lake grazing. A foal splashes and nips
at the adult horses. Awkwardly human, I wish invisibility,
but the horses have no interest in us.
They continue grazing, step out of the lake dripping,
their backs glistening under the afternoon sun.
They walk by casually, seeking other greens on land.
Watching them eat again, we remember we've missed lunch.
The horses grow more beautiful by the mouthful.

Remembering the Brown Recluse Spider

How it found its way under my shirt, I can't say.
Houdini-like, it slipped under my tight bra,
where it tasted the tender meat on the underside
of my left breast before rappelling down my belly's slope,
lingering on the vertical plane long enough to insert its fangs
again, leaving a second dose of potion without arousing
the body's pain sensors, not even a sting as minor
as a mosquito's bite.

It wasn't until evening, after showering, while drying
myself, that I discovered the holes where a spider
had drilled and tattooed urgent broadsides
in red, which kept turning brighter for nearly three weeks
before dimming and burning out. The first message
was in the simple language of a child. *I was here.*
The other spoke like a jilted lover. *Remember me.*

Where the Deer Slept

Today, chance led me to the place
where deer slept last night,
their bodies warming each other
on tall prairie grasses pressed flat.
Today, new snow covers
trees, houses, the road—
where the body of a buck lies still
on the median, his antlers small and useless.

It was just yesterday when I threw
peelings from apples for a pie
behind the house near the salt lick.
It was yesterday when a deer and her young buck
ate the apple skins and dry leaves before running
along the creek to cross the road.

Anagram for War

Each night I am raw with worry asking, *Why?*

From the radio and from helpers on the outside,
Anne Frank received the news, each day more Jews
being taken by force, arrested, removed.

She called herself *lucky* to have her diary,
lucky to see the sky, even from indoors,
lucky to breathe fresh air from a cracked window,
lucky to have food even when it was rotten,
lucky to call Peter her friend,
lucky for stolen kisses in the attic,
lucky until August 4, 1944.

In her diary she addresses her imaginary friend, Kitty:
Why am I among the fortunate,
safe in hiding while others disappear?

A girl in an underground bunker in Kiev sings "Let It Go,"
the Disney song from the movie *Frozen*. The song goes viral
and the girl has a moment of fame. Where is that girl now?
Is she alive?

Each night I am raw with worry as Putin weaponizes grain.
Each night I ask, *Why am I among the fortunate*
while others disappear?

The Norwegian Resistance Museum,
Akershus Fortress, Oslo

In deepest winter I think of her, an anonymous prisoner
and maker of handicrafts for barter. Because her real name
has been lost, I call her Martina after my great-grandmother,
whose mother came to America long before April 9, 1940.

Martina fashioned models of roofless houses,
floor plans recalled from an earlier life before the invasion.
Her gifts to the guards improved her prospects for food.
I picture her lying on her bunk, her narrow fingers
folding scraps as in origami, except she used trash,
not shiny squares. Except she made houses, not peace cranes.

Forming paper walls must have been soothing to her,
as she remembered the cozy rooms of her peacetime home,
as she walked her fingers down familiar halls
while eating smuggled food.

The Leafcutter Ants of Trinidad

1.
Thousands cross our path so that we clumsy birders
must leap over the moving snake of a trail they make.
Are they merely following a pheromone trail,
or does an ant general direct them?

They can strip a tree of its leaves overnight,
cut crescent leaf wedges in seconds with vibrating mandibles,
each piece up to fifty times their weight,
held in powerful jaws and raised up like green parasols.
The ants hurry the provisions home, deliver them to the grinder
ants who mash and feed them to the underground fungus
garden, future food and housing.

After fifty million years, the leafcutter ants have perfected
the art of community.

2.
Ukraine is broken now, says a man from Afghanistan,
shaking his head, heavy as stone.
After ten years working for the US Army at Kabul Airport,
he has enough English to tell some of what he witnessed.
Some things he may never tell.

Bricks toppled, tall apartment buildings bombed, crumbled,
always at least one side open, rendering them useless.
The electric grid ruined, water pipes broken,
bodies on the streets, others entombed below collapsed buildings.

We need a miracle to stop this war, to stop the murder of children
and civilians. And when it is over? We will need another miracle,
the human equivalent of leafcutter ants, to carry away the rubble,
to resurrect the art of community in Ukraine.

Putting the Roses to Bed

For the arboretum volunteer assigned to snip off rose blooms
and dig winter trenches to protect the most delicate flowers.
For the rose petals in a bushel basket decomposing.
For the loose petals that bring to mind weddings.
For the flower girl who took her job seriously and ran out of petals
mid-aisle, pivoting to return for more.
For the mother who signaled the girl to *keep going,
never mind the petals.*
For the mother who understood the difficulty of turning back
and never left her bad marriage.
For the volunteer who cut a red rose for one woman and a yellow
rose for the other.
For the volunteer who recalled the date two years earlier when
he put the roses to bed in the frozen ground beneath deep snow.
For the woman who went back to learn the name
of the yellow rose.
For the rose called Walking on Sunshine,
which the women did for days after the first snow arrived.

II.

Turning Pages

It is dawn when the recycling truck screeches to a halt,
the driver slight, female, young. She hovers over paperbacks
from our cart, old classics with pages too faded
even for the reuse store.

Here, we save words like gold, paper from banks
that might be failing and contracts, warranties, licenses,
receipts, all in coded language. Books crowd the shelves,
their poems and stories waiting to be heard,
even as another language somewhere in the world dies
every other week. So many words, but who hears them?

We keep trying to bridge the gaps with our words,
salmon swimming upstream to spawn,
shouting imperatives and questions that ricochet
between walls, cousins to musical notes
who give up their individuality, their names,
for the off chance of making a little music.

She stacks the books on the crook of her left arm,
carries them to her cab, like treasure. I wish
I could watch her tonight after her shift,
as she strains to read the faded print.

Rituals

My husband motions me out to the back deck
for a clear view of the salt lick by the creek.
After two hot July weeks, a doe and her spotted fawn
take turns at the white block. The mother is at home
here. When she's had her fill, she turns and begins licking
her fawn, grooming him so tenderly I remember he lived
inside of her only a short time ago.

I remember the summer baths our mother gave my sister
and brother and me at the cabin. We took turns sitting
in the metal laundry tub, Mother's body hovering
above, her washcloth dunked and wrung out again and again,
spilling warm water over our heads, water running down
her arms and soaking her blouse. She never minded getting wet.
She made it her mission to scrub the dirt from our skin.

When the fawn's mother stops grooming him, he turns
and begins licking her coat. What great imitators
the young are, registering all their parents do, learning
the best and the worst of us.

On the Occasion of My Birth

   after Meridel LeSueur

The sun rose at 8:07 and I entered the world at 8:38.
The moon waxed gibbous on this night before it grew full.
I was born female and my parents wanted a boy.
Already they had one girl, damaged in childbirth.
How long before I saw how my gender could offend,
could make others turn away?
How long before I saw the advantages it gave
to the other sex—to my brother?
How long before I was harnessed to the lowest,
recurring domestic chores, then to the most impossible
family work? My labors would never cure my alcoholic
father, could never cure my sister.

I was unformed and unwritten when I met LeSueur,
almost twenty-five and she nearly ninety,
wearing a squash blossom necklace too big for her tiny frame,
yet somehow just right. Her voice was deep and rough,
clear and strong. *Arise!* she called out to us,
women seated on hard folding chairs
in a dusty church meeting room in Minneapolis.
Her voice was a gentle gong that goes on ringing.

My Mother Was a School Librarian

In summer, my mother didn't read a single book.
She read women's magazines for their stories of love
and romance. My mother was a librarian who wore red
lipstick to work, where her quick smile moved her lips
up and down all day like a little drawbridge.

She wore dark, sensible shoes to work, her legs a blur
as she pushed book carts around her library. All day her hands
fluttered with purpose as she touched books, moving
them from counter to shelves and from shelves into the hands
of waiting children. Her hands flew as she stamped due dates
onto the cards she slipped into each book's pocket.
Sometimes a child would ask about a book missing
from its appointed place. Then, like the road runner
on the brooch pinned to her blazer, she would race
to the back room to find it among the books
waiting to be reshelved. My mother knew the series
each child was reading. She liked transporting children
to other lands to live, briefly, other lives.

My mother carried thousands of stories in her pretty, dark head.
On school days she dwelled in a world of words and tales,
our home as remote as a foreign country on a distant continent,
its name long forgotten.

Watching My Mother Smoke

She asks me to sit in my father's chair beside hers. His orange
chair is also velour, but it can recline. Mother listens better
when she is smoking. She hardly speaks at all. We sit together
mornings before she goes to work at the library
and before I catch my school bus. Sometimes we sit again
in late afternoon, if the house is quiet.

The hourglass salt sifts slowly to the other side.
When we sit in the orange chairs, I can tell her anything.
My friend smokes pot, *my friend* skipped school,
my friend is having sex.
She inhales deeply, with the intensity of a hummingbird
drinking sugar water in preparation for its migration south,
taking in as much as it can.

Tobacco feeds something deep in her.
She tilts her head back to release a cloud, smoky and sweet.
She is channeling passion I can't know.
We are still years away from her heart attack.
In a rare moment, she tells how she started smoking
in the first place, in protest of my father's drinking.

Mother's Five-Year Diary

for Sharon Olds

1946: Hold That Blonde, Somewhere in the Night, Weekend at the Waldorf, Fallen Angel, Stolen Life, Shy Pilot, Too Young to Know, The Harvey Girls, The Postman Always Rings Twice, Tarzan, Leopard Woman, Diary of a Chambermaid, Easy to Wed, Thrill of Brazil, Scandal in the Night, Two Guys from Milwaukee.

Mother's diary came into my hands after her sister died.
Early in marriage, Mom had left it in the custody of Rose,
who knew well of her longings and would keep it safe.
Rose said Mom was always boy crazy.

The small leather-bound book gives a page for each date.
Each page is divided into five spaces, with four lines for each date
from 1946 through 1950. The cryptic, cursive entries hint of
her varied love interests, hair washing, boredom, playing Canasta,
taking the long way home.

In 1946, my mother saw fifty-three movies, usually one
a week, though some weeks in spring she saw two.
On February 15, the weather foiled her plans:
Started to the show but had to turn back due to snowstorm.
The drive of someone deeply committed? Yes,
but to what—films? Or was she determined so young
to break free of the dirty, hard work of farm life?

The youngest of seven, each morning at 6:00 my mother
emptied the cows' udders while Rose helped their mother
in the kitchen. During threshing and harvest, Mother helped
in the fields too. Her entries on threshing days are brief,
her letters large and loopy, made in the delirium of exhaustion.

On Saturday nights, she luxuriated in other worlds: silk stockings,
cashmere sweaters, and trains. On Sunday mornings,
at the little church in Crary, North Dakota, there was time
during the sermon to review scenes from the night before.

In the part where Mom vacillates between her love
for Don and my dad, I think to offer words of encouragement
to move toward a stable life and faithful love. Then I remember
that my existence, my love, my kids, my poems, and my home
all hinge on her decision to marry my father.

1950: Great Lover, Chicago Deadline, Doctor and a Girl, That Midnight Kiss, She Wore a Yellow Ribbon, Silver Star, Heiress, Mighty Joe Young, The Jolson Story, Pinky, Battleground, Bride for Sale, Adam's Rib, Tokyo Joe, Dear Wife, Iwo Jima, Lady Takes a Sailor, Lucille Ball, Birdman, Christopher Columbus Came Early, Riding High, Gentleman's Agreement, Twelve O'clock High, Malaya, The Big Cat, My Foolish Heart, Broken Arrow, Bright Leaf, Duchess of Idaho, Canadian Rockies, Eagle and the Hawk, Mr. 880, Chamber Territory, Robin Hood.

It is Valentine's Day, 1950. The pages of Mother's diary
are nearly filled. He gives her a bracelet, a silk scarf, an orchid,
a corsage with pink carnations, a silver spoon, four hickies,
a couple of scratches, and a diamond ring.

On her birthday he gives her a cashmere sweater.
She loves him *so much she is scared.* She falls into his arms,
leans back the way Ginger did, trusting him to catch her.

Liza Lou's Kitchen

Rolling pin, eggbeater, kitchen sink, refrigerator, iron,
Tide, Joy dishwashing soap, Frosted Flakes, Captain Crunch,
cherry pie, toilet paper, a grocery list: sugar, butter, beer.
All of it is rendered in sparkling glass beads, monument
to women's labor.

On one side of the oven, Emily Dickinson's words:
She rose to his requirement
Dropt the playthings of her life
To take the honorable work
Of woman and of wife.

As a girl, I stood on one leg like a stork to make dishwashing
more challenging. My sister had the dish towel, but she hid
in the bathroom. My brother took out the trash.
Each night I rose to the requirement, lost myself in the warm,
sudsy water. Glasses first, silverware, plates, bowls,
until finally, the crusty pots and pans.

Too late, I say *thank you* to my mother for her kitchen
work. Too late, I say *thank you* to her mother, Emma,
who *worked out* at age fifteen, cooking, baking,
and washing dishes on another farm until her first baby
came at sixteen. And the babies kept coming, my mother
being the last of seven. Emma assigned kitchen work
to her daughters. My mother assigned it to my sister and me.

So long as we eat, we will labor in the kitchen.
Let there be dignity in the labor in every kitchen.

Note: Liza Lou, an American visual artist, created "Kitchen," a fully furnished kitchen made of glass beads. The monument to ignored women took five years to create. I first saw "Kitchen" at the Minneapolis Institute of Arts in 1996, then again in 2021 at the Whitney, New York City.

Early Photo of My Father

I study the photo of him in his mother's arms. Irene, small
and unsmiling, sits on the dock bench by the Wichita Reservoir.
Her dark bob and bangs frame her face. Her eyes are windows,
half-shaded, as if peering out ambivalently at her widening world.

She has crossed one leg over the other. Still, she appears like
a schoolgirl in her sailor's dress with its wide white collar
and dark bow. Are her hosiery and black lace-up pumps
attempts to look grown up?

Irene and Herman have traveled far, from Fargo
to Texas, to hide their predicament, my father born
too early to call him premature.
His father takes work selling Easy Vacuums door-to-door.
From Texas they announce his birthday exactly three months
later, on July 5. His birthday was always celebrated
on the Fourth of July with drinking and fireworks.
He learned of his true birthday while joining the Navy.

In the first months of my father's actual life, from April 5 to July 5,
what did his mother do when she couldn't stop his crying?
When he got croup?
When his bottom turned crimson?
When his father came home late from work? Far from home,
Irene could not ask his mother or hers for help.

Shame is like an air plant. It needs little to grow.
It breathes silently, eats and drinks silently, mysteriously.
When my father died, his sins and regrets were scattered
with his ashes. But his shame? Shame never dies.
It lives forever.

The Rat Snake

    after Jericho Brown

Serpent was the intruder her father once wed.
Now he shrinks in his narrow bed.

As he shrinks, she dwells on the words he once said.
Words to betray are the words that betray him.

Betrayal was his usual way, not a passing whim.
The rat snake, confused, is known to eat his tail.

Her father is spent, too tired to speak or wail.
At the end, he is saddled with all the things he bought.

At the end, betrayal means you're finally caught.
Her father asks her to cover his feet and toes.

He asks her to pull the covers right up to his nose.
Her father is shrinking in his narrow bed.

Her father pulls up his covers until she sees only his head.
Serpent was the intruder her father once wed.

The Genealogist and Horses

My grandfather willed my mother a horse.
My great-grandfather willed my grandmother a horse.
My father's father raced horses but never owned any.
My father had no horses, being a city fellow, so I learned
to ride on my cousins' horse. Each time I was bucked
off, my cousins laughed. *Get up! Get back on the horse!*
And I did, until finally that horse let me ride.

I used to dream of my father leaving me a horse
to show the love he couldn't express.
If not that, as a symbol of his wish to love.
But my father had no horse to give.

My Father's Circles

He walks his bones early to late, behind his silver
cart. When tired, he circles his bed like the dog
who wants to select the best spot.
One day he is in trouble with the law.
Another, he has a new job making lots of money.
He is perplexed by the many things he has acquired,
can't keep track of them all, opens wide
his closet doors to show off his bounty.

His decisions have all been made.
Inside which circle will his path end?
The windows keep out most sounds, though not
the muffled voices of visitors in the car park,
and never the echo of barking dogs.

She Liked to Tell Strangers She Was Adopted

She would lift her shirt to show her belly,
which housed no divot or button, all the proof
she needed to claim she'd been adopted.

Her power grew in proportion to her strangeness.
Surely, she sensed this. By twelve she was large,
brutish, fearsome, yet she never harmed me, her little sister.

Her stomach was wide and held a thin line of a scar,
almost invisible, formed by hernia repair.
Of course, she once had an umbilical cord

linking her to our mother, until it was cut at birth.
After that, she lived like an astronaut floating
out in space, unreachable.

Lost Days and Nights, Part I

When the sheet of lined yellow paper appears, it has already
lived a long and difficult life. It wears crinkles instead of folds,
is stained with dirt and food, coffee or blood.
The recorder has used a crayon to make thick hatch marks
in groupings of four, a diagonal line through each, as in a tally.
At the bottom of the page, three lines stand alone. I puzzle
over the marks until their meaning comes clear:
This is a record of days spent in prison by a man unable to read
or write, my sister's boyfriend. She loved him and he loved her,
but in rage he often hurt her, blackening her eyes.

The yellow paper is saved, moved from apartment to apartment
along with dishes, pots, and pans. I find it on moving day,
recall iron doors clanging shut, my body frisked
years before, while visiting her in prison.

She is gone now, but I keep the yellow paper in mind.
And I keep a tally of my lived days, etched on the inner husk
of my skull, knowing that at any moment one can wake
in a place where time dissolves.

Lost Days and Nights, Part II

In Florence, beneath the Medici Chapel, Michelangelo's
hatch marks are etched in stone on the wall of the room
once his cell. I linger by the cold, damp wall.
This small chapel is where Michelangelo hid himself
for three months after siding against his patrons,
after the pope put a bounty on his head.
This is where he set his gaze on an imaginary horizon,
where he let his eyelids droop until his cell became atelier
so that he could work again. Here, he drew scenes
from the Sistine Chapel, made a new self-portrait,
and sketched ideas for future paintings.
While counting his lost days, Michelangelo
answered the promise of art.

Like Conjoined Twins

I breathed for myself and for my sister, a lonely girl
who hid in her basement bedroom, garish in its red
carpeting and red velour bedspread.
There, she soothed herself, ate entire jars of pickles,

spilling the sweet juice onto the carpeting, where ants
came to feast. Her bedroom was another country,
a world I could not enter, place to cultivate imagination
and grow her appetite for solitude, place to masturbate.

One expects kindness from teachers. What a shock to learn
that not every teacher means to be kind. As we practiced vaulting
the horse in gymnastics, our teacher shouted,
The horse should be riding you!

My sister looked to me for doses of love until she departed
home for the dangerous world, in search of romantic love.
Meanwhile, my heart kept beating the only way it knew,
double time, prestissimo, prestissimo.

This Is the Story of a Stranger

Strange, and yet surely I knew her and her story,
how it could fill books of philosophy and religion,
especially the stories where they cast out the homely,
the lonely, the lowly, the ones without. Look
how we go on praising and raising
those already in possession of money, talent, success
while my sister waits at a bus stop on Penn Avenue.

I did not recognize her at first, windblown.
She was large, but it seemed the wind might topple
her. The imitation leather sack purse,
hanging on one shoulder, had often served
as receptacle for partial rolls of toilet paper
from the clinic or wherever else the bus took her.
She stole at Thanksgiving dinners, secreted teaspoons
back to her apartment where I found them later
while helping her to move apartments.
If it was the first of the month, her purse held cash.
From one wrist, a plastic bag dangled. Bewildered
was how she looked. Bewildered I remain.

Did I stop to ask, *Where are you going?*
Can I give you a lift? I kept driving south,
maybe to the mall. *Was it her? Was it really her?*
I'd seen her worse, still I clung to my disbelief.
What misfortune, hers. What misfortune, mine.

Long Shadows

Remember using your hands to make birds fly and bunnies hop?
Dog, wolf, alligator, butterfly, a mouth talking.
You can be short even as your shadow stands tall. Figures lean
together, jump, stand, or wait at the threshold.
They walk away or follow. Did you ever try to take a photo
only to find you couldn't keep your shadow out of the frame?

When I was a child, my sister always followed me. Later,
she moved in and out of my life, casting flickers of darkness.
Once I traveled to the Philippines thinking
I would be out of her shadow, finally.
Climbing the holy mountain, I thought of her.
Cooling myself under a waterfall, I thought of her.
Near the Cave of Judgment, eating rice from banana leaves,
she sat in our lunch circle, along with warrior ghosts.

Her dying took twenty years. After her last breath,
I touched her cooling hand, felt her soul depart.
Her long shadow remains. It waits in doorways.
It waits on street corners.

American Sonnet, the Body

Perhaps the body wants to linger, to live
after the mind has flown, after the soul has departed.
Near the end comes the time of questions,
yet without conception of the final approaching hour.
So tired is the beloved, as if to seem eager, almost, for relief,
and not yet thinking, *What can it mean? What will it mean?*
There is the long day and the long night, the clock
turning. Then the moment just before the last.
Oh, stillness of that frozen moment.
Oh, body stooped over the bed as the final breath departs,
onward ever silent. Then comes the rapid cooling of skin,
limbs graying and stiffening, body of the huge, stubborn life,
the life that once demanded everything.

Elegy for My Sister

When you were alive,
I was also more alive,
my life always on emergency.
I lived like an ambulance
driver, exceeding every
speed limit. I was an officer
holding you at bay
with my fake gun
and sometimes with a plea bargain,
or, rarely, logic. I was a firefighter,
beating down pop-up flames.
Each day arrived with its new agenda.
I never had to think what to do next.
Each day, after breakfast,
I would turn on my siren
and spinning lights. Each day,
I would speed down the highway
to a street address just given to me,
the city of my destination yet unknown,
forever unknown.

Love Poem for North Dakota

Once in a while a long truck passes us,
carrying the wing of a windmill, a big ant
lugging a giant white moth. There is nothing
much to look at. The trees, sparse before Fargo,
are rare now. Our great-grandparents were keen
to find such rich soil to yield corn, wheat, sugar beets.
I doze and wake in my brother's blue time machine.
We are going to the funeral of our favorite aunt, Rose.
Fifty miles from Grand Forks, a field of gold,
then another and another: rows and rows of sunflowers.
Thousands, all turned toward the sun.
I imagine us long ago, two small figures standing in a field,
not yet knowing the meaning of the word *future*
or how its shadow would keep growing shorter and shorter.

III.

Sonnet for Time

Say you believe it can be saved, so you set out
to collect its remnants, stray seconds and minutes.
Say the clocks explode all at once, illusions of plenty
dissipating to dust. Say in the moment you begin
to grasp its scarcity, you try to buy more, then discover
it is never kept in stock.
Say it does not improve when pressed or worried:
It is meant to be worn casually, like linen.
Say you try tipping onto heels to relive the past
and strain on tiptoes to glimpse the future.
Say it waits patiently while your heart goes ticking down,
stretches during sickness, like rubber. Say in the dim hours
counting your blue jumping sheep, it is Time who
unlatches the gate, freeing them to graze the meadow.

The List

after James Tate

The list is as long as a python, as heavy as the anaconda,
and as slippery as a water boa. It seems harmless like a garter
or corn snake, both known for gentleness,
but the list was never harmless, not even in the beginning.
Some weeks it goes silent, like the hognose snake
who plays dead instead of lashing out.

Nothing slithers away from my *To-Do List.* In fact,
more things slide onto it daily: scan photos, clean out files,
alphabetize spices, reduce my carbon footprint.
Occasionally, I find the time and nerve to work on an item
from the list, but I never completely finish a task,
never put it to bed, so it can't be crossed out.
Priorities change, the items get scrambled.
It looks different, but it's the same list.

Like the colorless ghost snake of Madagascar, the list haunts.
It might go quiet for a while, or even get mislaid
among advertising flyers, bills, and receipts,
but I know it's lurking.
Always I'm thinking: If the things on that list
aren't completed pretty soon, or at least by the time I die,
I'm going to give up.

Artifacts

Under files, fortune telling cards. Behind them, a miniature toy
bus, a jeepney, from the Philippines. On the wall, Robert Hass's
broadside, *The Problem of Describing Trees.* In a stack, notebooks
holding the dead ends of genealogy. In a basket,
cords and chargers for devices gone to landfills.
On a shelf, Mother's five-year diary. In drawers, worn files,
transcripts, résumés, recertifications. Every bookshelf spills
over, the thickest and newest books by Ann Morrow Lindbergh
and Nelson Mandela have unbroken spines. Here, writing
gets done when the frenzy of modern life subsides for a day.
Here, spiders build trapeze lines, unseen until a sunny day
like this one when they glisten and sway to the rhythm
of the furnace.

Who will care for these books after I'm gone, especially those
signed by Lucille Clifton *For Mary, Joy?*
Who will dare to throw out the giant atlases, *The History
of North Dakota* and *They Chose Minnesota?*
Who will discard photos and baby books? My brother?
My husband? My children? Who will love these words
as I love them, here, where visiting cats curl by my desk?
Here, where the dead and the living reside together in love.

Clothes on the Line

I am a young mother again, carrying wet clothes and linens
in a wicker basket, hanging them on lines in our narrow,
fenced backyard in Minneapolis, where tall delphiniums
and daisies grow. I slap the wet sheets with relish,
taking out the folds. My son loves playing hide-and-seek
between the rows, his safe cloister under the warm sun.
You have to pin a clothespin just so to catch the edges
of two shirts or diapers at once.
By now nearly everyone in America has a clothes dryer.
So do we, but I like hanging laundry out to dry.
At bedtime I breathe in wind saved in the sheets.

In Italy, I take dozens of photos of laundry:
lingerie and men's underwear by the sea, Porto Venere.
Blue jeans out windows, Florence. Bedsheets on long lines
in *la campagna.* Bras hidden in the middle row, Borseda.
The Italians seem quaint, if a little backward,
yet I have begun to question something we call progress
back home.

Microchimera

Your children are not your children.
They are the sons and daughters of Life's longing for itself.
                                        —Kahlil Gibran

No goat's body or lion's head, no tail of a snake, but surely I am
less feminine after raising sons. I watch sports and swear,
and I imagine their Ys alongside my Xs.

Right away they got comfortable and took what they needed
without regard for my teeth or bones, without regard
for my comfort. Some of their cells and blood invaded,
traveling across the placenta. When each fetus departed,
I knew it was time. I think of them casting off their cells
the way teens drop clothing. Were they merely absent-minded
or were they intentionally leaving gifts?

The second child, two weeks late, was reluctant to leave,
but I bet he took some cells left by his brother,
along with some of my cells and some grandma cells.
He may have even taken cells left by the brother conceived
before him, the one who died in utero,
and left cells for the future he could not meet.

One day, when I am deathly ill, my children—the born
and unborn—may provide the stem cells to help me recover
from some illness I can't yet name. I won't have to ask
for help. Their cells surely lurk in the tissues
of my cesarean scars or in my bone marrow, liver, kidneys,
or heart. They might even reside in the neurons of my brain.

My children are not my children. I know that.
They belong to eternity, and they carry our family tree.
My womb was their first home, the place they lived
and grew just below my heart.

My Suspicious Breast

It is June when the hydrangea flowers blossom into pale globes.
Meanwhile, my right breast is held at knifepoint.
I review the history of my breasts—training bras, padded bras,
athletic bras, push-up bras, breast exams, and the caresses
they've enjoyed since age sixteen. I was lucky to be endowed,
or so everyone said. But when they first grew, I wanted to hide
them like secret love letters whose author I could not reveal.
No matter how hidden, the boys' eyes found them fast, like iron
filings to a magnet, as if they could see through my clothing
to the bullseye nipples underneath.

In youth, my nipples were like headlights, pointing straight ahead.
Now they are always in a state of confusion, looking
in any direction, but mostly down.

Once an insistent bra clerk in a changing room scolded,
Bring them up, up.
They were tired from nursing babies, who used to pull away
from the nipple with a slurp, suddenly sated, to stare at me
with love-glazed eyes, the milk breast left out in the open.

While I once wore low-cut dresses and tops, I now consider
the benefits of having small breasts, boy-like, with flat nipples,
or no breasts at all. My breasts have become as challenging
as difficult children. *Hard to read,* says the doctor,
who describes their *architecture* as *distorted,* then sends
me to the hospital for 3D pictures that give no new information.
My breast continues in its suspicious ways and must be probed
with long needles.

When the hot days of June have passed, the calendar turns
over to July and doctors tell me to return to my life.
There is no cancer, no need for worry.

But I am an experienced doubter, slow to let down my guard.
Even as age and gravity tug at my old breasts,
they remain my own soft, plump pillows.
I will keep them for as long as I can.

Oropesa, Spain, Where Pilgrims Once Slept

Face pressed to the gift shop window,
I ponder how many handkerchiefs
with hand-stitched
yellow and red flowers
and bluebirds I could use.
How many will I give away?

I ask for four.
Why not six or eight?
Poverty, my faithful mule,
has followed me here.
I have made weightier decisions,
poorer ones too.

Working a corner of the linen
between thumb and forefinger,
I grieve the handiwork
left to other buyers,
exquisite uniform stitches,
luscious threads of silk.

A thousand times and more
small white flags
have waved
in surrender
to my life as it is,
and to all it is not.

Husbands

   for Wendy

Another died last night, giving his wife a new name, *Widow*.
A man can be a husband one day, fixing the snowblower
or retrieving his son from the police station, and a ghost
the next. The same husbands who go to work on Mondays,
when they might rather lie in the hammock,
may depart suddenly, as a distant sinking boat shimmies
down at sea. How could *he,* who made everyone laugh,
whose smile was a lighthouse beacon, leave without warning?

One friend found her husband cold in the morning.
At bedtime he was still her lover, his eyebrows lifting
with his questions. By morning all his questions had flown.
The two would bike together mornings at a bird sanctuary.
Now she pedals their old route alone, solitary
as a migrating hummingbird.

One woman I know woke in the night when her husband's heart
stopped. She called 911 and took instructions by phone,
pumping his chest wildly, the soft mattress swallowing him.
And his heart answered. It began again.

I don't want to suffer like the widows I've known,
don't want to celebrate my husband's birthday with emails
from friends or grow stronger and more self-sufficient in the face
of death. I don't want to recall the woman I was in my youth
or preserve his unwashed work shirt to use as my pillow
infused with his scent. If ever I am tested,
let me be like the one who knelt on the mattress,
the one with animal strength that brought her husband
straight back from the dead.

In the Therapy Pool

There were four of us, old women, on that cold morning,
two hanging from bright-blue noodles, one water-walking,
and me wearing a baby-blue life belt in the deep end.
She appeared, then descended the ramp slowly, cautiously.
Our four heads turned, and not soon enough
did any of us manage to look away, her beauty
wholly unexpected. She towered above us on long legs,
stunning in her bikini, a white bottom and a peach top.
Her hair was blond, her skin without a scar, blemish, or cellulite.
Was she an apparition? Daphne? Sappho?
The ghost of my sexual past only taller and prettier?
At the end of the ramp, she fell backward to wet her long
tresses. Now I could see she wore a pale pink lipstick,
though no other makeup. The four of us wore one-piece suits.
There was Greta in pink, with her cropped hair, Maria in floral,
Radha in her purple suit, faded and frayed from chlorine.
I wore a black one-piece, my hips and feet hinged and fastened
now with screws and titanium. I thought of the times I'd scolded
my husband for looking at other women. She turned,
went to the opposite side of the ramp, and why not?
We were clearly from another tribe.
She lay on her back, a lime-green noodle beneath her neck.
Only her face and rib cage floated above the surface,
a stretch I could no longer achieve under
any circumstances. Having finished
the last 120 reps for my abs, I ascended the ramp.
Halfway out of the water, dripping, I stopped
to stretch my calves. There she was, right beside me,
her nose narrow, delicate in its straightness.
I thought of my younger self, the past a distant mountain
from which I'd descended. I thought of my lust,
how troublesome it had once been. Gone now.

No, not gone, but deeper, muted. I thought how
I'd take it back without hesitation, like a truant lover.
Look how the body inevitably betrays desire,
makes it new, no longer a runaway train.

The Painter in His Studio

> for the Minneapolis Institute of Art (MIA)
> and for painter Albert Launay, 1884–1903

He will keep working in his studio, his painting forever
in progress, his brushes upright as he holds a palette
in his left hand. His right hand will always be brushing
aside his black coat jacket, seeking refuge in his dark pocket.
The woman in the green dress will keep smiling,
her dress forever tied at the shoulder with a silly bow.
Another woman, whose face will remain a mystery,
will wear the same red, flowing dress from now until eternity.

What are you doing? asks a docent in training, rustling
her black taffeta skirt. *We're writing. We'll put you in our story.*
We laugh and the woman moves away, forever shadow to our joy.
The painter keeps his white handkerchief in his left pocket. Only
his collar reveals the white shirt he wears beneath his jacket.
His hat looks similar to a bowler hat, only not quite. Is it a hint
of the power he wishes were his?

If I could step into Launay's painting, I would smile
like the woman in the green dress and floppy hat
with a big yellow flower to one side. I would be the woman
with pleasure on her lips, her mouth open, her head tilted
back, nothing like the woman I am today,
dressed in black, reading the day's obituaries.

At the Butterfly Museum

The blue morpho butterfly lights on my head for so long
that it seems to have become part of me.
Though the butterfly's legs tickle, I resist the urge to scratch.
This blessing won't be with me for long.
The blue morpho looks like a different butterfly when its wings
are closed. Then it shows mostly brown, with some spots
encircled in turquoise and yellow.
Its blue brilliance shows only when it is flying.
When it closes its wings and rests on a leaf, you have to search
to find it, camouflaged, its beauty folded inward.

Dog Park, Ocean Beach, San Diego

Some of us throw frisbees and slimy tennis balls to huskies
and German shepherds, to dachshunds and pit bulls, to Labrador
retrievers and cocker spaniels, to bulldogs and Weimaraners.
Soon we are smiling. The dogs mostly play chase, stopping
to sniff each other's privates, turning again to meet the gaze
of their owners, as lovers would. It is still early, but the sun
ascends quickly. Two dogs ride surfboards,
though never over a wave's crest. Who could feel sad
watching dogs float on surfboards on the sparkling expanse
of the ocean?

We're calm and smiling by the time we begin walking
in deeper sand. Maybe we're kinder too. You'd think war
hadn't been invented yet, that slavery played no part in our history,
that homeless people weren't wrapped in sleeping-bag cocoons
where the pavement meets sand. When a dog nips at my son's dog,
apologies come easily from both sides. Forgiveness is granted.
We're shoeless. Our stomachs rumble. A woman has forgotten
to bring a bag for her dog's poop. No worries.
A woman in a canary-yellow T-shirt offers one.

Back home in Minneapolis, protestors occupy the city streets
again. Last night Daunte Wright was killed by police.
He was twenty. His name replaces another name at the top
of a long list of victims. Did I really believe
there would be no more police killings?
I struggle to hold the growing list of the dead.
They won't walk any dog to any park. And Mr. Wright?
He won't walk again with his son, who at age two
is only beginning to understand that his father is gone forever.

It Keeps Happening in Minneapolis

in memory of Amir Locke

At Bolero Flats there is a sundeck on the seventh floor,
a basketball court, an indoor swimming pool, a fitness center,
clubhouse, business center, skyway access, gated, controlled entry.

You think you're safe, but here the police enter with a no-knock
warrant. Nine seconds later, Amir Locke is dead.
Two bullets to his chest, one through his wrist. A guest
at a cousin's place, he sleeps on the couch under a white quilt.

No time for coffee or a run now. No time for a pickup game.
No time to lift weights. No time to call his mother. No time
to call his father. No time to fly back to Dallas.
No time to start the music business of his dreams.

No time is dying time.
The sun is coming up.

The officer turns the key slowly. We watch it
again and again, as we watched George Floyd's death
for months and years. We cannot grasp what the police
do in our names, shouting *Get to the floor!*

No time for waking, no time to get to the floor
or drop the gun Amir holds in sleep,
without a finger on the trigger. We watch,
each time shuddering, our pain a dust mote
to the suffering of Amir's loved ones. We know little,
only that we want the killing to stop.

The Eagle Cam

Through the terrible month of February, unable to glimpse
the end of winter, we watch and wait as the parents take turns
sitting. We watch as the father accidentally cracks one of two eggs.
We watch, remembering last year's eaglets, living in the same nest
until the larger sibling pushed the runt to its death. We watch,
remembering how some parents have eggs that never hatch,
yet they keep sitting well beyond the incubation period,
glacially slow to accept their loss. Then, finally they circle
overhead before starting over, though the female
may not be ovulating anymore.

We watch as heavy snow falls on the birds,
the fierce wind adding to the burden of sitting day and night.
Once, a storm leaves a foot of snow covering the mother:
She never leaves the nest. She shakes, lifts her wings
until her head sits above the white blanket.

Sometimes we watch television, the bombed-out buildings
in Ukraine, exhausted soldiers, the nuclear power plant
at risk, everything gray. Always we return to the eagles' nest.
Watching makes us hopeful, like good grandparents who live
next door to be of help in ordinary ways.
Watching is pure oxygen for us,
our world now a hazard of wind, weather, and fire.
We don't know when the war will stop, or if it ever will.

We are like these birds. We know what it means to add
new mistakes on top of our old ones. At one time
or another, each of us has built a nest on a rotted branch,
launched into the wrong career, or married the wrong person.

Every year for twenty years different eagle couples
have added a few hundred pounds to this nest,
the branch dying sometime along the way.

Just before the biggest snowstorm arrives, the two
add more feathers, leaves, and sticks.
The heavy falling snow adds more weight.

The winds grow stronger, the nest sways. The mother's
back feathers lift, her eyes dart side to side.
She flies as the nest descends, all 2,000 pounds
of it, landing upside down.
After finding and nudging the eaglet's body,
the two circle above. They will likely nest again,
but not until next year.

Sugaring

Blue bags hang from our trees to collect the sap we boil
down to syrup for waffles and pancakes, maple popcorn,
and grilled salmon. Every day for a month
I've touched each of our thirty-one maple trees.

We are still learning, my husband and I, sugaring
this second year. The work has changed me:
One afternoon my lips graze the rough bark
after adjusting a tap.

Under some of the trees, I find fresh deer pellets.
Nearby, tall grasses are pressed flat for bedding.
At night the deer stand on their hind legs to lick
the bark's rivulets for spilled sap.

The Small Paintbox of April

The one that abides the lingering cold,
that's the one we love.
Our love arrow flies to the heart
of the pansy, its petals not delicate,
though they seem to be, its petals
painted gold and purple and blue.

In May we will love other blooms,
our hearts suddenly reckless, our windows
opened wide, for the waft of lilacs and peonies,
for the glimpse of daffodils, for the tulips
cheering the dull landscape. Now we have
only the promises of the varied greens, weeds
equal to all except the precocious pansy.

Mother, the hummingbirds arrived

after a long and bitter winter, after Putin's murderous spring.
We wake to the orioles' songs you knew by heart. To see
them we must be clever, for they are wary of us.
At night, the barred owls deliver us to oblivion.

Mother, in this time of bird flu, we are forbidden
to put out seeds for the hungry birds. We still offer sugar
water to the orange birds you loved and to your green
hummingbirds. The flu is now in the foxes too.

It would be impossible to name all you've missed, Mother,
my children and grandchildren. My grief sleeps but never dies.
I carry my longing with me wherever I go, but Mother,
the hummingbirds arrived after a long and bitter winter.

Dark Night with a Strawberry Moon

Even with the full moon, it is too dark to see
the deer passing through the yard
on their way to Purgatory Creek. We sip
iced tea on a deck above. Our ice cubes
melted over an hour ago.
We shush each other to listen
to their approach, as if it will give us news.
How did they winter over?
Are they hungry? Thirsty? Pregnant?
They reveal nothing.
Yet, we are happy to have them near
as they rustle last year's leaves
on the forest floor. It is June in Minnesota.
The wild strawberries are ripening.

Like labor pains

the disasters come closer together now.
Fires, icebergs melting, snow cyclone bombs,
extinctions. We're in deep, in need of each other,
in need of every kindness. When the cock crows,
I turn over to reach for him.
When the cock crows, I set down my dread,
refusing to be like John Berryman, without hope,
without feathers. When the cock crows,
I lift Berryman back onto the bridge, where he forgives
his father's suicide, where he gives up his despair.
I take his hand and you take mine. Our fear
of the future transforms to a hawk flying into blue.
We don't let go. We never do.

Love All of It

Love the mutt's expression full of all he can't tell,
and the jagged chunks of ice floating on the lake.
Love the one with the wound exposed in the bitter cold
and the one who ran for help, a little too late. Love the seed,
safe, although that seems impossible in the dead of winter.
Love the shadow of the eagle, large but brief,
and the wren who is small yet equal to the eagle.
Love yourself naked or in your plain clothes.
Or in your sick bed near the end, going over everything,
memories of your life rushing in, full of noise
in that quiet room.

About the Author

Mary Junge learned about sun dogs and prairies in childhood while living in Fargo, North Dakota, before moving to the Twin Cities with her family. After earning a bachelor's degree from Bemidji State College, she settled in Minneapolis and worked as a teacher of young children while earning a master's degree in educational psychology from the University of Minnesota. Soon she found herself drawn to poetry. For ten years she was a member of the Laurel Poetry Collective, based in St. Paul, Minnesota, under the leadership of Deborah Keenan, a professor at Hamline University and a teacher at the Loft Literary Center.

Travel experiences have been transformative for Junge since she was a young adult, providing a doorway to other cultures and places. Quilting is another of her passions. The slow speed at which fabrics are pieced together enhances her writing life.

Junge's poems have been published in numerous journals and anthologies: *Art Word Quarterly, bosque, Crosswinds Poetry Journal, Dust and Fire, Laurel Poetry Collective publications, Oyster River Pages, 2023 Red Wing Poet Artist Collaboration Anthology, Sidewalks, Split Rock Review,* and *Water~Stone,* among others. She previously published two poetry books: *Express Train,* a chapbook (Pudding House Publications) and *Pilgrim Eye* (Laurel Poetry Collective).

Deep gratitude to some of the many master poets who have provided inspiration and solace: Eavan Boland, Jericho Brown, Gwendolyn Brooks, Lucille Clifton, Natalie Diaz, Mark Doty, Rita Dove, Louise Glück, Linda Gregg, Robert Hass, Terrance Hayes, Joy Harjo, Jane Hilberry, Edward Hirsch, Jane Hirshfield, June Jordan, Ted Kooser, Meridel LeSueur, W.S. Merwin, Pablo Neruda, Naomi Shihab Nye, Sharon Olds, Mary Oliver, Gregory Orr, Tracy K. Smith, Ruth Stone, James Tate, and Natasha Trethewey.

Thanks to the Loft, a literary center in Minneapolis, and to teachers of poetry in the Twin Cities: Margaret Hasse, Deborah Keenan, Roseann Lloyd, Jim Moore, Thomas R. Smith, and Joyce Sutphen. Thanks to my generous and kind mentors Roseann Lloyd and Deborah Keenan. Thanks to Sean Hill and the Northwoods Writing Conference, Bemidji. Thanks to Ellen Bass, James Crews, and Danusha Lameris for online classes during the pandemic. Thanks to the Key West Literary Seminars, especially workshop instructors Jane Hirshfield, Rowan Ricardo Phillips, Kevin Young, and Tyehimba Jess.

Thanks for restorative, inspiring writing residencies: Norcoft, Minnesota (RIP, Joan Drury); Ragdale, Illinois; the Rensing Center's outpost in Borseda, Italy, especially Ellen Kochansky.

Thanks to my many generous friends and peers who have supported me with interest and encouragement. Thanks to New York poet friends Cathy Wald and Sheila Rabinowitz and to Wanda John-Kehewin, a poet living in Vancouver, B.C. Thanks to Jacqueline Trimble and Katherine J. Williams, poets from Key West workshops.

Thanks to Pegatha Hughes, an early writing partner. Thanks to Dara Syrkin, poet and wordsmith.

Thanks to my stellar poetry group: June Blumenson, Kate Green, Shannon King, Sandra Larson, and Carol Rucks.

Thanks to the Laurel Poetry Collective, especially our initial organizer, Deborah Keenan, a brilliant poet and legendary teacher.

Thanks to the Painted Chair Poets: Shelly Getten, Sharon Hilberer, Barb Jones, Sandra Larson, Bo Lee, Roseann Lloyd, Ilze Mueller, Mark Stuart, and Pam Wynn.

Thanks to Vicky Lettmann and Joyce Kennedy for ongoing support and feedback about poetry and life. Thanks to my children, grandchildren, my brother Mike, and my cousin Donna for their encouragement and enduring love. Thanks to my mother, who remains with me always. Thanks to my husband, Mark, for everything.

www.ingramcontent.com/pod-product-compliance
Lightning Source LLC
Chambersburg PA
CBHW030910170426
43193CB00009BA/799